Looking for Jack

Written by
Stephen Rickard

Illustrated by
Beatriz Castro

ished in 2026 by
wood House Press
4 Clinton Street
o, NY 14224

d in the United States of America

Library of Congress Cataloging-in-Publication Data:
Names: Rickard, Stephen, 1957-, author. | Castro, Beatriz, illustrator. | Sanchez Ayala, Richy, illustrator.
Title: Looking for Jack / written by Stephen Rickard, illustrated by Beatriz Castro. The Max Beebnut / written by Stephen Rickard, illustrated by Richy Sanchez Ayala.
Description: Buffalo, NY : Norwood House Press, 2026. | Series: Phonics all-stars: phase 3 |
Identifiers: ISBN 9781978577992 (pbk.) | ISBN 9781978578005 (library bound) | ISBN 9781978578012 (ebook)
Subjects: LCSH: Reading–Phonetic method–Juvenile literature. | English language–Phonetics–Juvenile literature. | Moths–Juvenile literature. | Friendship–Juvenile literature. | Social media–Juvenile literature.
Classification: LCC LB1573.3 R534 2026 | DDC 372.465–dc23

CPSIA compliance information: Batch #CW26NHP: For further information contact Norwood House Press at 1-800-237-9932.

Carl is feeling sad. His pet, Jack, is missing.

Carl is looking for Jack, but he cannot see him.

Is Jack chilling in Carl's bedroom?

No.

Is Jack zooming in the living room?

No.

Sasha and Jeff will look for Jack with Carl.

"We will get him," Sasha tells Carl.

Sasha, Jeff, and Carl look for Jack.

They all look in the bedroom.

They look in the garden.

Sasha and Jeff cannot see Jack.

"Look! I can see Jack," Carl tells Jeff. "He is sitting on the light."

They all look at the light.

Sasha looks at Carl. "Is Jack a dog?"

"No! Rex the dog is not missing," Carl tells Sasha.

"**This** is Jack. Jack is a moth!"

The Max Beebnut

Written by
Stephen Rickard

Illustrated by
Richy Sanchez Ayala

Chuck was sitting in the coffee bar.
He was waiting for his dish of eggs.

It had been a hard week.

The waitress got the food for Chuck.

Picking up his fork, Chuck dug in. The dish was good!

Then a man sat with Chuck.

The man was looking at Chuck. He was looking at his dish too.

Looking up, Chuck had a big shock.

The man was Max Beebnut, the
big-shot king of You Noob, on the web.

Max Beebnut was the best.
Yet Max Beebnut was in this coffee bar, with Chuck! It was nuts!

Then Max took a fry off Chuck's dish and, with a dip in the egg ...

Pop! He bit it.

Giving Chuck an odd look, Max got up.

"You can tell your pals that you met me, but they will not think it was me. Not **the** Max Beebnut, not in **this** coffee bar."

Then Max quit the coffee bar.

Chuck got up to go. He had to tell his pals he had met Max Beebnut.

But Max was right.

Not **the** Max Beebnut, not in **this** coffee bar.

With a quick look, Chuck sat. Picking up his fork, he dug back in to his eggs.